1000 MONSTER JOKES for Kids

Please look after this monster

Frank N. Stein

WARD LOCK LIMITED · LONDON

Other titles in this series:

1000 Jokes for Kids
1000 More Jokes for Kids
Oh No — Not Another 1000 Jokes for Kids
1000 Limericks for Kids
1000 More Amazing Facts for Kids
1000 Howlers for Kids
1000 What's What Jokes for Kids
1000 Crazy Jokes for Kids
1000 Stoopid Jokes for Kids
1000 'Orrible Jokes for Kids

© Ward Lock Limited, 1987

First published in Great Britain in 1987
by Ward Lock Limited, 8 Clifford Street,
London W1X 1RB, an Egmont Company

Cover cartoon by Roy Mitchell

All other cartoons by Heather Clarke

Text set in Plantin
by Rapidset & Design Ltd., London WC1

Printed and bound in Great Britain
by Collins, Glasgow

British Library Cataloguing in Publication Data
Stein, Frank N.
   1000 monster jokes for kids.
   1. Wit and humor, juvenile   2. English
   wit and humor
   I. Title
   828'.91402'0809282   PZ8.7

   ISBN 0-7063-6576-3

Contents

This book is dedicated to all my monstrous friends, especially Doctor Frank N. Stein who screwed me up!

Frank. N. Stein

Hellarious Humour

What has fangs, is hairy and is 2 metres tall?
  A 4 metre werewolf bending over to tie his shoelaces!

Believe it or not, the Bride of Frankenstein ran off with a moose—Frank has just received a *Deer* John letter!

It's a known fact that young werewolves always do well at school. Whenever they're asked questions they give snappy answers.

How do we know the devil is bad-tempered?
  He always seems hot under the collar!

When the dead souls were making too much noise shovelling coal, Satan started screaming, 'What's all that *hell*abaloo?'

NEWS FLASH

Count Dracula has just run off with a giraffe. He fell madly in love as soon as he saw her neck!

Where do zombies pick up their mail?
  At the dead-letter office.

You can always trust a mummy not to give away secrets—they keep their knowledge under wraps!

What do you get if you cross a mummy with a vampire?
  A flying bandage.

What is Dr Jekyll's favourite game?
  Hyde-and-seek.

Mother ghost to child: 'Remember what I taught you—only spook when you're spooken to.'

Ghosts love music—especially haunting melodies!

When American ghosts take a vacation, where do they go?
  To resort areas around Lake Erie.

How does a ghost count?
  One, BOO, three, four, five, six, seven, eight, nine, frighTEN.

One female spirit has just got a job with British Airlines. She's an air ghostess!

What do you call a female spirit who is very fat?
  A ghostess with the mostess.

Who has the most dangerous job in Transylvania?
  Dracula's dentist.

Contrary to popular belief, Dracula never got married—he remained a bat-chelor.

Ghosts are considered to be cowards—after all, they have no guts!

People who study mummies often have problems because they get too wrapped up in their work!

Before he could testify in court, Dracula's dentist had to swear to tell the tooth, the whole tooth, and nothing but the tooth.

What's an Italian ghost's favourite food?
  Spook-etti.

How do you kill an elephant that's been bitten by a werewolf?
  You have to shoot him through the heart with a silver peanut!

When ghosts feel like a beer, what pub do they go to?
  The Horse & Gloom.

Name the most famous monster detective of all time?
  Sherlock Gnomes.

What do monster cannibal children love to eat?
  Human bein's with boiled legs.

Name the unluckiest monster of all time.
  The luckless Monster.

Ghost: I have a terrible cold with a very bad sore throat.
Doctor: Take some coffin drops.

What do you find in a haunted cellar?
  Whines and spirits.

How do young spooks prefer their eggs?
  Terrifried!

Most vampires are known to be simple-minded. After all, they're all suckers!

One invisible man passed another invisible man and said, 'Hello, it's nice not seeing you again.'

What's the difference between an elephant and a stupid monster?
  A stupid monster never remembers.

What red meat does Dracula despise?
  Stake (steak)!

A vampire went through life with only one fang—he had to grin and bare it!

'Doctor, doctor—I keep thinking I'm the Invisible Man.'
  'Who said that?'

Did you know that priests often think of ghosts as spiritual members of the community?

What did the boy zombie say to the girl zombie he loved?
  'Darling—you really kill me.'

An automobile manufacturer once tried to cross a vampire with a Volkswagon. He wound up with a monster machine that attacked luxury cars and sucked out their gas tanks!

One stupid vampire cracked both his fangs. He'd never heard the old saying, 'You can't get blood from a stone,' and kept trying to bite a rock!

What do you use to flatten a ghost?
  A spirit level.

Did you hear about the invisible little girl who wanted to be a gone-gone dancer when she grew up?

What do you call the overweight ghost who haunts the opera house?
  The Fat-tum of the Opera.

What kind of horses do zombies ride?
  Nightmares.

Teacher: What is a skeleton?
Pupil: Bones with people scraped off.

It has nine eyes, two noses, three mouths and four ears. What is it?
  Ugly!!

Where do zombies swim?
  In the Dead Sea—where else?

What do you call a drunken ghost?
  A methylated spirit.

Why do ghosts like to haunt tall buildings?
  Because there are lots of scarecases!

In which western American town might you find thousands of zombies?
  Tombstone.

Did you hear the ghost rooster this morning?
  It woke me up with it's spook-a-doodle-dooos.

Cross a witch with an iceberg and what do you get?
  A cold spell.

What happened to the author who died?
  He became a ghost writer.

What is green, loves peanuts and weighs over two tonne?
  A little green elephant from Mars.

Why is the air especially clean and healthy to breath on Hallowe'en?
  Because so many witches sweep the sky.

Where do zombies go for their jokes?
  To crypt writers.

What's the favourite subject of young witch children?
  Spelling.

'But mummy—I don't want minced meat again for supper.'
  'Shut up and put your legs back into the meat grinder.'

What's the marching song of monsters?
  Gory, Gory, Hallelujah . . .

What did the Invisible Man say to his girl-friend?
  'Cynthia—you're really out of sight!'

Why do young couples go to see horror films?
  Because they love each shudder.

What do ghosts love to chew?
  Boooble gum.

Why are vampires completely crazy?
  Because they're all bats.

What's even more invisible than the Invisible Man?
  The Invisible Man's shadow.

*What's the difference between a tiny witch and a deer that is trying
to run away from a hunter?*
  One's a stunted hag, the other's a hunted stag.

What type of plates do skeletons eat from?
  Bone china.

What's a vampire's favourite dance?
  The Fangdango.

Young Frankenstein loves to read—especially stories with a
cemetery plot!

In which book do the names of famous ghosts appear?
  Booos Who.

How do ghosts travel when they go abroad?
  By British Scareways.

Where did the devil go to replace his lost tail?
  To a retail shop.

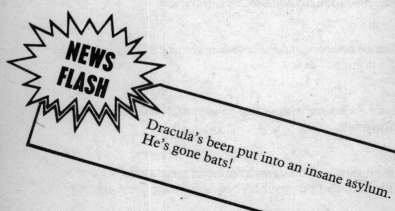

NEWS FLASH

Dracula's been put into an insane asylum.
He's gone bats!

Look at that poor little ghost walking on crutches—you might say he's a hobblin' gobblin'.

Interviewer: In your opinion who was the most beautiful woman in history?
Satan: Without a doubt, it was *Hell*en of Troy!

'Mummy, Mummy—I just caught a green monster—what should I do?'
    'What can you do—wait until it ripens!'

What should you do with a blue monster?
    Make an effort to cheer it up.

I just heard that young Dracula loves soup—his favourite is Alpha*bat* soup!

What do young monsters love to eat?
    Ice-scream.

Harry: Do you know what monster is the fastest eater?
Larry: Of course—it's the goblin.

Cross a Brontosaurus with a Venus's fly-trap and what do you get?
    A monster plant that eats elephants and rhinos.

What is the wicked old woman who lives by the sea called?
    A sandwitch.

And if she refuses to go swimming during rough seas, she's known as a chicken sandwitch!

A wicked witch named Daisy
Just sits—she's very lazy.
    She has no cares,
    She sits and stares,
Some claim that Daisy's crazy!

When ghost trains travel across the country, where do they stop?
    At manifestations.

People keep canaries and parrots as pets. What do ghosts keep?
    Booo-jies!

What is Dracula's children's favourite game?
    Bat's cradle.

What do you get if you cross a Brontosaurus with a kangaroo?
    Holes in the ground.

What do you get if you cross a termite with a Brontosaurus?
A monster bug that eats through skyscrapers for breakfast.

When's a turkey like a ghost?
When it's a goblin'.

What type of dog does a ghost have?
A *booo*dle.

Do you know what the Abominable Snowman loves to eat?
It's cold-cuts!

What do you call a fat Abominable Snowman?
An Abdominal Abominable Snowman.

MONSTER TONGUE TWISTER

Say ten times quickly—*Abdominal Abominable*

When do werewolves argue?
When there's a full moon—they fight tooth and nail!

Satan is a man who has to do lots of soul-searching!

Dracula is thought of as truly a *die*namic individual!

What's the best way to make friends with a werewolf?
Buy him a box of dog biscuits and a fat juicy bone.

Name the American city famous for its wicked old ladies.
Witchita, Kansas.

Mary: What did you think of the film we saw about the Abominable Snowman?
Ivan: It left me completely cold.

Jeff: How can I stop a werewolf from attacking me?
Mitch: Don't panic—just pick up a stick, throw it as far as you can, and yell, 'Fetch, boy, fetch!'

A werewolf is the one animal that's never around when you want him. You always have to call 'Where wolf? Where wolf?'

Frankenstein was very talented. You might say he was a man of many parts!

'When Dr Frankenstein makes monsters, does he get paid by the hour?'
   'No—he does piece work!'

Did you hear about the poor old lady who had a heart attack while hanging out her laundry?
   Believe it or not, one of the sheets just flew away!

Two monster armies were facing each other. What was the land between them called?
   Gnome-mans land.

That's the Spirit

What's on a ghost's bicycle wheels?
  Spoooks!

'I heard a ghost talk last night.'
  'What did it say?'
  'How should I know—I don't understand dead languages.'

How can you tell when a ghost is about to faint?
  It goes as white as a sheet.

Why did the Invisible Man keep looking into the mirror?
  He wanted to make certain he still wasn't there.

What monster discovered electricity?
  Benjamin Franklinstein.

Which piano is used most often by monster pianists?
  A Franken Steinway!

When I was a little boy, all the kids called me four eyes. Then
I got a pair of spectacles and all the kids called me eight eyes!

What do you get if you cross a cow with Tyrannosaurus Rex?
  A bovine monster that eats anyone who tries to milk it.

The art of spying on a ghost is known as Peeka*booo*!

Are jokes about Satan funny?
  They're **hell**arious!

What do you get when you cross a flower with a fire-breathing monster?
A snapdragon.

When the devil needs assistance, what does he yell?
Hellp!

How does Satan travel?
By **hell**icopter.

What do werewolves eat for snacks?
Ladyfingers—**real ones**!

What do you get when you cross some bread with peanut butter and a werewolf?
A hairy peanut butter sandwich that howls when the moon is full.

Werewolf: Last week I had a lovely guest for dinner.
Dracula: Did you enjoy having her?
Werewolf: She was more than just enjoyable—she was absolutely delicious!

What's Satan's favourite amusement at the fairground?
The **hell**ter-skelter.

Cross a vampire with a midget and what do you get?
A monster that sucks blood from people's kneecaps!

Jim: Do you know what English sea monsters have for lunch?
Slim: Of course—fish and ships.

What's pink, has a curly tail, lives in a pen and drinks blood?
A hampire.

What's a sure sign that a werewolf has raided your refrigerator?
Paw-prints in the butter.

Do you know what happened to the Egyptian pharaoh who ate crackers in bed?
He became a crummy mummy.

MONSTER TONGUE TWISTER

Say ten times quickly—*Crummy Mummy*

When ghosts need medication, what pharmacy do they visit?
Booots (where else?).

What is made of metal with hair all over, and can move through the air at over 1000 miles per hour?
King Kongcorde.

What did the monster mum say to her child at dinner?
How many times do I have to tell you not to talk with both mouths full!'

'Mummy, Mummy—what's for breakfast?'
'Shut up and get back in the frying pan.'

'Mummy, Mummy—Daddy's going out.'
'Well, don't just stand there—help me shove him back into the oven!'

What do you call an outer space monster with thirty eyes, ten ears, four noses and three mouths?
Sir!

Why did the outer space monster decide to give up boxing?
He didn't want to ruin his good looks.

How do ugly old women tell the time?
They use a witch watch.

MONSTER TONGUE TWISTER

Say ten times quickly—*Witch Watch*

What's Dracula's favourite song?
Fangs for the memory.

'*Why don't you like Dracula?*'
'Because he's a pain-in-the-neck!'

Why did the idiot monster lose his job as a lift operator?
He couldn't remember the route.

What do short-sighted ghosts wear?
Spook-tacles.

What should you do it you see a skeleton running across a busy road?
Jump out of your skin and join him.

When Dracula visits New York city, what's his favourite skyscraper?
The Vampire State Building.

16

It started to rain so daddy ghost told his little ones, 'Put on your **booo**ts and ghoul-oshes.'!

What do monsters eat for breakfast?
   Dreaded wheat.

If a spirit likes sailing, what should he join?
   The Ghost Guard.

What is Dracula's favourite sport?
   Bat-minton.

Why did the monster go to an astrologer?
   He wanted to see his **horror**scope!

What did one ghost say to another ghost?
   'I simply don't believe in people.'

'Doctor, doctor—I think I'm invisible!'
   'Who said that?'

What sort of children does a monster florist have?
   Bloomin' idiots.

What did Dracula say to his last victim?
   'I am a vampire—go and wash your neck!'

Knock! Knock!
Who's there?
Frank.
Frank who?
Frankenstein!

Name the skeleton that was Emperor of France.
Napoleon Bone-apart.

NEWS FLASH

King Kong's just been rushed to hospital. He's had an attack of ape-pendicitis!

Why couldn't Dracula eat school dinners?
He was afraid of getting a steak (stake) through his heart.

Why couldn't the skeleton pay his fare on the bus?
He was skint!

What's the difference between a wizard and the letters M. A. K. E. S.?
One makes spells and the other spells makes.

What do monsters eat for lunch?
Ghoulash!

How do ghosts pass through locked doors?
They use a skeleton key.

What do pixies do after school?
Their gnomework.

When the monster kid saw Santa Claus, what did he say?
'Yum, yum!'

Why did Dracula visit the dentist?
He had terrible fangache.

What do you call a stupid skeleton?
A numskull.

Why is a monster bachelor so smart?
Because he's never Miss-taken.

Which monster musicians can never be trusted?
The fiddlers.

What happened when the Abominable Snowman fell out with his girl-friend?
She gave him the cold shoulder!

19

What's another name for a young monster who's a butcher's boy?
  A chop assistant.

Why do monster firemen wear red braces?
  To hold up their trousers.

What do vegetarian monsters eat?
  Swedes.

Two giant monster spiders met and fell in love. The day they married they became newly-webs!

What do you call a monster snake that works for the government?
  A civil serpent.

What has feathers, fangs and goes quack?
  Count Duckula.

What did the monster say to his female victim?
  'I've got a crush on you.'

Did you hear about the monstrous fat cat?
  It drank 100 saucers of milk and set a new lap record.

What do you call a monster camel with three humps?
  Humphrey!

What's big, green and sits in the corner all day?
  The Incredible Sulk.

Did you hear the joke about the monster in the quicksand?
  It takes a long time to sink in!

Why did the one-handed monster cross the road?
  To get to the second-hand shop.

Why are ghosts invisible?
  'Cos they wear see-through clothes.

What did one witch say to another witch?
  'Snap, cackle and pop!'

Where might you find a prehistoric monster cow?
  In a **moo**-seum.

What do you call a monster moth?
  A mam-moth.

Did you hear about the monster chicken?
  It keeps using fowl language.

Why does a giant monster mouse need oiling every day?
  Because otherwise it squeaks very loudly.

Why was the ghost arrested?
  It was haunting without a licence.

What newspaper was read by dinosaurs?
  The Prehistoric Times.

Architects who designed the pyramids told the pharoahs, 'We guarantee satisfaction or your mummy back.'

How do you keep a monster from smelling?
  Cut off his nose!

In one sense, Dracula is like a beggar—he's always trying to put the bite on people.

When the giant monster walked through a potato field, what did the farmer end up with?
  A harvest of mashed potatoes.

When is Dracula not a vampire?
  When he turns into a street.

A monster cannibal walked into a restaurant and ordered the waiter . . .

He also wanted some soup with a full-bodied flavour . . .

'What about beans?' asked the waitress. 'Would you like some beans?'
  'Of course,' answered the monster cannibal—'Human bein's.'

A ghoul fell down a well and died. You might say he kicked the bucket!

What do you call a mistake made by a ghost?
  A **Booo-booo**!

What's worse than being bitten by Dracula?
  Having to shake hands with Captain Hook!

When the lights went out, where was Dracula?
  In the dark!

What kind of ants are 10 metres tall?
  Gi**ants**!

Did you hear about the obese monster cannibal who went on a diet?
  Now he only eats pygmies.

What did the witch say to her small broom?
  'Go to sweep, wittle baby.'

'May I haunt your castle?' asked the spirit.
  'Certainly,' answered the king. 'Be my ghost.'

Cross a warlock with a millionairess and what do you get?
  A rich witch.

MONSTER TONGUE TWISTER

Say ten times fast—*Rich Witch*

Cross a snake and a funeral and what do you get?
  A hiss and a hearse.

Cross a parrot with a shark and what do you get?
  A monster animal that could talk your ear off.

What a Scream!

What's Satan's favourite dessert?
   Devil's food cake.

What type of sweet does young Dracula love?
   An all-day sucker.

NEWS FLASH

King Kong has just been married. The monster world is sending him their Kongratulations!

'Can you tell the difference between King Kong and a banana?'
   'Of course—a banana is yellow!'

It's said the Invisible Man is a very poor liar—after all, anyone can see through him.

Andrea: Is it true that monsters won't hunt you if you carry a torch?
Ivan: That depends on how fast you carry it!

What's the scariest letter?
   G—because it turns a host into a ghost!

What's Dracula's favourite stone?
   A tombstone.

If you listen closely, you can hear zombies speak in a grave voice!

What did the skeleton say when he received a comb for Christmas?
   'Thanks—I'll never part with it.'

What's the favourite colour of ghosts?
   Booo (blue).

Host ghost: My girl-friend is a medium.
Guest ghost: Really? Mine is a small.

MONSTER TONGUE TWISTER

Say the following words ten times fast—*Host Ghost*

Do you know why Dr Jekyll goes to Miami beach every winter?
   To tan his Hyde (hide).

Name the famous vampire composer?
Bat-hoven.

What happened to Bat-hoven after he died?
   He stopped composing and started decomposing!

What farm object do ghosts love to watch?
  The scarecrow.

The next time you see a zombie, notice the expression on his face—it can best be described as dead-pan!

Did you hear about the female ghoul who went on a strict diet?
  She wanted to keep her ghoulish figure!

Where do American Indian ghosts sleep?
  In a creepy teepee.

MONSTER TONGUE TWISTER
Say the following words ten times fast—*Creepy Teepee*

Do you think zombies enjoy being dead?
  Of corpse they do!

What does the monster hangman read at breakfast time?
  The morning noosepaper.

Nurse: Doctor, doctor—the Invisible Man is in your waiting room.
Doctor: Tell him I can't see him now!

Why does Dracula wear a black belt?
  To keep his trousers up.

How do you disguise a mummy?
  With masking tape.

How do you say 'monster' in French?
  'Monster in French'!

MONSTER TONGUE TWISTER
Say the following words ten times fast—*Guest Ghost*

What flies in the night and goes 'Flap, flap, chomp, ouch!'?
  Dracula with a sore fang.

What is a mummy after it's 5000 years old?
  5001 years old—what else?

What do ghouls eat for breakfast?
  Shrouded wheat.

Cross a skeleton with a jar of peanut butter and what do you get?
  Bones in your peanut butter.

'Do you know what's purple and eats people?'
  'Of course—a purple people eater!'

MONSTER TONGUE TWISTER

Say ten times quickly—*Purple People*

What do you call a skeleton who stays in bed all day, every day?
  Lazybones.

Which ghost specializes in haunting clocks and watches?
  The spirit of the times.

What kind of raincoat does a monster wear on a rainy day?
  A wet one!

Interviewer: Tell me—why do you ride on a broomstick?
Witch: It beats walking.

Why do ghosts travel in lifts and on escalators?
  To raise their spirits.

What happens when a mummy overeats?
  He gets a tombie-ache!

How can you make two mummies out of one?
  Make him so angry that he's beside himself.

What did the mummy think of the stone statue of a lion?
  He said it sphinx!

Knock! Knock!
Who's there?
I sphinx.
I sphinx who?
I sphinx I've got the wrong house.

A mummy caught fire—he became the last of the red hot
mummies!

How do you treat a sick monster?
  With the utmost respect.

What day do monsters like best?
  April Ghoul's Day.

*When two vampires reach a victim at the same time, what's it
called?*
  A neck-tie.

Where does the Abominable Snowman go to dance?
  At a snowball.

When two abominable snowmen fight, what's it called?
  An icebox!

*When the Abominable Snowman got married, where did he go on
honeymoon?*
  To Miami beach—where he melted!

*What do abominable snowmen say when they return from
holiday?*
  'There's snow place like home.'

If you don't believe in Cyclops be careful—you're making a
big myth-take!

Why were the two Cyclops always fighting?
  They couldn't see eye-to-eye!

What's it called when Cyclops get together for a big dance?
  An eyeball.

What's a monster's favourite drink during a heat wave?
  Ice-ghoul lemonade.

Boy: Did you ever see anyone who looked like me?
Girl: Yes—but it cost a lot of money to get into the freak show.

Cross a chicken with a ghost and what do you get?
A peck-a-**booo**.

What did the young woman say to Dracula?
'You're starting to get under my skin.'

What should you do if you think you've been bitten by a vampire?
Drink some water and see if your neck leaks.

Which musical is the all-time favourite of monsters?
My Fear Lady.

What did Dracula say as he bit into the neck of Santa Claus?
This is really going to sleigh you.'

Did you hear what happened when a boy ghost met a girl ghost?
It was love at first fright.

What's Dracula's favourite breed of dog?
A bloodhound.

When Dracula leaves his coffin, what time is it?
Time to run!

Which monster headed the government of France?
Charles de Ghoul.

'Mummy, Mummy—how do you make a monster stew?'
'Keep it waiting for at least three hours.'

What do ghouls love to drink?
Tomb-ato juice.

When young monsters are about to go to sleep, what do they like to hear?

A gory story.

MONSTER TONGUE TWISTER

Say the following words ten times fast—*Glory Gory*

Why can't a monster's nose be twelve inches long?
Because then it would be a foot.

What do you call a monster that chases an entire rugby team?
Hungry!

There goes King Kong—he looks ape-alling!

What's the best way to talk to King Kong?
Long distance.

What did Satan's girl-friend tell him when he helped her out of the rain?
'Darling—you're an angel.'

How does the monster, Bigfoot, impress people?
He puts his best foot forward.

Did you hear about the monster who needed an operation?
He had his ghoul stones removed.

Which monster makes strange noises in his throat?
   A gargoyle!

Cross a policeman with a ghost and what do you get?
   An inspectre.

Did you hear about the midget ghost?
   He's too small to use a sheet; instead he has to wear a pillow case!

A female ghost couldn't control her young daughter. She said, 'I can't do anything with her—she's such a spirited girl.'

What kind of make-up do female ghosts use?
   Vanishing cream.

What type of car does Wolfman drive?
   A Wolfswagon.

The mother monster was annoyed as she served dinner to her son. She said, 'How many times do I have to tell you—don't eat with both mouths full!'

Boy Meets Ghoul.

A monster male brought a female home and said to his mum, 'This is Carol—she's my new ghoul-friend.'

What's the best thing to do if you find a ghost in your bed?
  Run!

Why did the monster boy kiss the monster girl on the back of her neck?
  He had to—that's where her lips are!

What spirit was a great painter?
  Vincent van Ghost.

The Bride of Frankenstein knows how to scare peeping Toms. When she undresses she leaves the curtains open!

Why was the ghost thrown out of the wine bar?
  They didn't serve spirits after 11 p.m.

What song is top of the monster's hit parade?
  'Thank heaven for little ghouls.'

One skeleton told his friend, 'Soon it's going to rain—I can feel it in my bones.'

Where do baby monsters come from?
  Frankenstorks.

One female ghost just got a job as a *boootician*!

What does an Egyptian monster call his parents?
  Dead and Mummy.

Where do clever young monsters go to?
  Ghoullege.

Who was the great ghost escapologist?
  Booodini.

What skeleton was a famous detective?
  Sherlock Bones.

What did the ghost writer say?
  'I only write when the spirit moves me.'

Grandpa Dracula told his son, 'The dentist gave me a pair of false teeth, but I hate those new-fangled devices.'

NEWS FLASH

News has just come in that Dracula has become a blood donor!

What did Dr Jekyll's nurse say to the patient?
  'Please have a seat. The doctor will be with you in a moment—he's just changing.'

It was an old missionary who gave a tribe of cannibals their first taste of christianity.

What do you find in an elephants' graveyard?
  Elephantoms!

Why do skeletons frighten easily?
  Because they don't have any guts.

A bolt of lightning struck Frankenstein. He smiled and said, 'Thanks—I needed that.'

What's it called when monsters get together and march for a cause?
  A demon-stration.

What did the old skeleton complain of?
  Aching bones!

Young Dracula brought a monster home and said 'Father—this is a fiend of mine.'

Frankenstein was looking at a newspaper and said to another monster, 'I love to read all the current news.'

What did the monster tell his sweetheart on Christmas Eve?
  'Best vicious of the season!'

Dracula saw a lovely woman pass by and said to Wolfman, 'I've always been a sucker for a pretty face.'

What's a female monster's favourite song?
  Demons are a ghoul's best friend.

What do ghost parents tell their children?
  'Don't spook until you're spooken to.'

What game do ghost children like to play?
  Haunt-and-seek.

Sign on cemetery gates:
DUE TO THE STRIKE, GRAVES WILL BE DUG BY
A SKELETON CREW

When female mummies get together to discuss fashion, it's called a wrap session.

The Bride of Frankenstein told him, 'Darling—I have a monstrous headache.'

Definition of a skeleton: A nude nude.

Mummies can always be trusted to keep a secret—they know how to keep things under wrap!

A mother skeleton told her little boy, 'Drink up your milk—it's good for your bones.'

Why didn't the spirit like to join in athletic contests?
  He felt he didn't have a ghost of a chance of winning.

Dracula told his mother, 'Stop nagging me—you're driving me bats!'

Why did Dracula bite the dentist?
  He started getting on Dracula's nerves!

The ghost was a great football player—some say he was *spook*tacular!

How did skeletons send each other letters in the days of the wild west?
  By the bony express.

Have you seen Wolfman's latest girl-friend? She's a real dog!

How long did the ghost plan to stay in London?
  Not long—he was just passing through.

A female ghost told her best friend, 'Many years ago I married a skeleton—and he's made a rattling good husband.'

Wolfman told Frankenstein, 'I don't like my dentist—he's so boring!'

Why do ghosts hate rain?
  It dampens their spirits.

Why do monsters prefer to eat natural foods?
  Because they're gnome-grown!

The spirit on guard duty heard a noise in the night and said 'Halt—who ghosts there?'

Satan was once overheard saying, 'It's a hell of a life!'

Zombies can often be heard making cryptic remarks!

What happens when a mummy has a bad cold?
  It starts coffin!

What skeleton was Emperor of France?
  Napoleon Bone-apart.

Dracula's wife said, 'When I fell for Dracula it was love at first bite!'

What flowers do monsters grow?
  Mari-ghouls and mourning gorys.

What do you call an attractive ghost?
  Boootiful!

What do spirits eat for breakfast?
  Ghost toasties, with **booo**berries and evaporated milk.

What's a skeleton's favourite instrument?
  The trombone.

Young spirits love to go to playland and ride on the roller ghoster!

What does a monster chef enjoy cooking most?
  Gnomelettes!

When Dracula goes out on a date with a woman he always feel like necking!

Teacher: Today we're going to learn about Cyclops.
Student: That's a good eye-dea!

What is monster children's favourite bedtime story?
  Ghouldilocks and the three pall-bearers . . .

And when they get a little older, the children read all about Ghoulliver's Travels.

There's now a new trend in horror films—the monster gets the girl!

Kids today are different—now they go to horror films and root for the monster.

Dracula is a person who becomes jocular when viewing a jugular.

Dracula is definitely a pain-in-the-neck.

A graveyard romance begins when boy meets ghoul.

Dracula fell in love with a female vampire, but they couldn't get married. You might say they loved in vein.

'Mama, Mama—all the children at school say I look just like a werewolf.'
　'Shut up and comb your face.'

What did Baron von Frankenstein say to his monster just before he brought it to life?
　'Lie down quickly—you're going to be in for a shock.'

Baron von Frankenstein completed his monster by making a bolt for his neck. Then, as the monster started to get off the table, the Baron made a bolt for the door!

What's the most common disease of old skeletons?
　Arthritis!

Have you heard about the two-headed monster at the circus who went on strike for higher pay?
　He claimed he had an extra mouth to feed!

What's on the front of a beauty magazine for monsters?
　The cover ghoul.

When a bunch of werewolves get together they usually have a howling good time.

There's a new Dracula doll. You wind it up and it bites a Barbie doll on the neck.

What do you call a warlock from outer space?
　A flying sorcerer.

Did you hear about the midget witch who was so small she had to fly around on a whisk broom?

What did the Invisible Man call his mother and father?
  Transparents.

A little German monster shoved his mother over the cliff then turned to his friend and said, 'Look Hans—no Ma!'

What's the normal eyesight for a monster from Mars?
  20-20-20-20-20-20-20 vision.

A huge monster with eight arms and nine legs walked into a tailor's shop. 'Quick,' said the owner to his assistant, 'hide the free alterations sign.'

The Frankenstein monster thought to himself, 'I just know it's going to rain today. My nuts and bolts are giving me hell!'

Did you hear about the ghost who listened to too many stories about humans and scared himself half to life?

Mother skeleton to her daughter: 'Eat a little more, dear—you're beginning to look like a bag of bones.'

Why didn't the old skeleton want to go to the party?
  His heart wasn't in it.

Young Frankenstein got a new chair for Christmas. He was so thrilled—he could hardly wait to plug it in!

PLUG NOT INCLUDED

Dr Jekyll confessed, 'I used to be a werewolf but I'm all right noooowwwwwww!'

Why did Frankenstein go to see a psychiatrist?
  He was feeling a bit screwy!

Winnie may have been an old witch but she still had charm!

What sort of transportation does a sorceress use?
  Witchcraft.

If an Egyptian mummy had back problems, who would he contact?
  A Cairo-practor.

'How did you like the new monster film?'
  'It was terror-ific!'

What did the naughty young mummy do that was wrong?
  He wrote dirty hieroglyphics on the pyramid walls . . .

. . . When his father heard about it he said, 'Tut, tut.'

Young ghosts should be heard—not seen!

I've heard that when Dracula goes to sleep he sometimes has horrible bitemares.

What do you call a motorcycle owned by a witch?
  A brrrrroom stick!

Not many people know this, but when Dracula was a boy he had to wear braces—the poor kid had bucked fangs!

What's so surprising about coffins?
  People are dying to get into them.

Wolfman is one of those men who leaves no stomach unchurned.

If a skeleton needs a check-up, what kind of doctor should it see?
  An orthopaedic specialist.

Dracula took his ghoul-friend to the theatre. After the show, he took her for a bite!

Why did the skeleton refuse to go to the disco?
  Because he had no body to dance with.

What would you say to a monster child that you haven't seen in several years?
   'Well—you certainly have gruesome.'

Dracula's wife said to him, 'You don't look well—your eyes are all bloodshot.'

When her monster husband came home late, the Martian housewife shouted, 'Where on earth have you been?'

Vincent Price was an actor who played in many horror films. He became successful beyond his wildest screams!

What did the Egyptian doctor say as he finished bandaging the mummy?
   'Well—that about wraps it up!'

Why did the Invisible Man's son want to be a hippie?
   Then he'd really be out of sight.

You're In For a Shock

'*What part of the horror film scared you the most?*'
  'The part when I ran out of popcorn.'

If you open your door and see Dracula, Wolfman and Frankenstein, what should you do?
  Pray it's Hallowe'en!

What's top of the monster Hit Parade?
  What kind of Ghoul am I?

Dracula said to Wolfman, 'I hate to be the one to tell you this, but you look like you're going to the dogs!'

'Mummy, Mummy—I hate Daddy's guts.'
  'Just leave them on the side of your plate and eat the rest.'

Cross a vampire with a hyena and what do you get?
  An animal that laughs at the sight of blood.

The young monster said, 'When I become old enough to marry, I'm going to look for a ghoul just like the ghoul that married dear old Dad.'

The Abominable Snowman would always toss three people at a time into the icy water. He did this because his mother told him that, 'Two's company, freeze a crowd.'

> ST PETER'S MOTTO
> Hear no devil, speak no devil, see no devil.

What do skeletons fear most?
A pack of hungry dogs.

MONSTROUS THOUGHT
Beware of Satan or evil have his way.

What is Satan's children's favourite holiday?
Hellowe'en.

Satan's children are real little devils . . .

. . . Just like their father, the kids have that devil-may-care attitude.

Did you hear about the missing monster whose whereabouts is ungnome?

Where does Mr Hyde usually go for his holiday.
To Jekyllslovakia.

Forgetting about the time, a werewolf went to a barbers for a haircut. Soon the moon came out and the haircut wound up costing him a fortune!

What does every werewolf suffer from?
Five-o'clock shadow.

'What seems to be the problem?' asked the doctor.
'I'm not sure,' said the monster, 'but I keep feeling that people are staring at me.'

'Dr Jekyll, tell me about your other self.'
'Beat it—you're getting under my Hyde.'

How does a zombie begin a letter?
'Tomb whom it may concern . . .'

What did the corpse say as the undertakers lowered his coffin into the wrong hole?
'You're making a grave mistake.'

Tombstone to corpse: I'd like to take you out.
Corpse to tombstone: Over my dead body.

A group of zombie dancers are known as a corpse de ballet . . .

. . . You might say they're completely *dead*icated to their art.

The television show about spirits was shown ghost-to-ghost.

We know very little about ghosts—they're shrouded in mystery.

First society ghost: What do you think of the new season's shrouds?
Second society ghost: I wouldn't be seen dead in them.

If a witch stays at a hotel, she'll probably ring for b-room service.

A sign at a witches' gathering read:
WE CAME
WE SAW
WE CONJURED.

When twin babies are born and one is a witch, it's hard for the mother to tell which is witch.

How do baby witches cry?
Brew-hoo! Brew-hoo!

Did you know that most mummies prefer embalmy weather?

Why did Godzilla decide to eat Tokyo instead of Rome?
    He discovered that Italian food gave him indigestion.

When it comes to American Indians, Dracula prefers the ones that are full-blooded!

Name a Hollywood actor who saw a ghost and didn't even turn a hair.
    Kojak.

What does the Abominable Snowman wear on his head when he goes outdoors?
    An icecap.

As a young child the witch did poorly in school—she could hardly spell!

Why did King Kong join the marines?
    He wanted to learn about gorilla warfare.

What's the best way to get King Kong to sit up and beg?
    Wave a 500 kg banana in front of his nose.

Young Dracula: What's a dentist?
Dracula: Just think of her as a filling station.

Dracula's wife claims a dentist is someone with a lot of pull.

Dracula thinks of children as his own flesh and blood . . .

. . . He's always happy to have another child. He says, 'I like to feel I'm bringing new blood into the business.'

What does Dracula go to see every year?
    The Hearse of the Year Show.

Why did Dracula leave the small village so quickly?
    He claimed it was just a one-hearse town.

Where does Dracula keep his savings?
    In the blood bank—where else?

Dracula recently received a letter from the bank's manager saying his account was 200 litres overdrawn.

What kind of car does Dracula drive?
    A bloodmobile . . .

. . . and he can get at least thirty miles to the pint.

Did you hear about the time Dracula was driving back and forth on the motorway searching for the main artery?

Dracula is a man of fashion—he's always dressed to kill!

To a man like Dracula, modern plumbing is hot and cold running blood.

The Abominable Snowman went to a football game and kept himself cool by sitting next to the fans.

What does the Abominable Snowman order at MacDonalds?
  Icebergers, with chilli sauce.

What kind of boats do vampires travel on?
  Blood vessels.

Dracula is a man who receives enormous amounts of fang mail.

Teacher: Who can tell me what those giant monster-like dinosaurs ate?
Student: Judging by the skeletons I've seen in the museum, they didn't eat much.

Two vampires were answering letters from members of their fan club and one said to the other, 'Do you mind if I borrow your vein? Mine has just run out of blood.'

One night while Dracula was out west paying a flying visit to American Indian tribes, he flew over the Grand Canyon and thought to himself, 'Isn't that *gorges*!'

Famous words of Dracula: There's a sucker born every day!

How can you make a witch scratch?
  Take away her W.

When Dracula tells a story you can be certain it's a pretty bloody yarn.

When Dracula first started writing poetry, things went from bat to verse.

Why did all the skeletons in the cemetery stare at Adam?
  Because they'd never seen a skeleton with one rib missing.

What did Adam say when the other skeletons teased him?
  'Come on guys—stop ribbing me.'

Witch in hospital: I feel a lot better today.
Doctor: You're coming along very well. Perhaps tomorrow you'll be able to get out of bed for a spell.

Satan went into a fish restaurant—he ordered fillet of soul (sole)!

A ghost came home very late one evening and gave his wife an excuse. She said, 'Don't try to fool me with that ridiculous story—I can see right through you!'

There's a new Dracula film containing lots of funny bits. It's being advertised as a comedy of terrors.

One female vampire who was an actress didn't take a job for a long time. She claimed she was waiting for a special part—one she could really sink her teeth into!

'Mummy, Mummy—why do I keep going around in circles?'
  'Shut up or I'll nail your other foot to the floor.'

The Bride of Frankenstein went to the dentist. He examined her and said, 'My dear, you have acute pyorrhea.'
  'Never mind the compliments,' she replied, 'just take care of my teeth.'

How does the Invisible Man look?
  Like nothing you've ever seen before.

What is a blood count?
  Count Dracula.

MONSTER TONGUE TWISTER

Say ten times quickly—*Bugs Blood*

Witch: Do you ever get frightened?
Skeleton: Never—nothing could make me jump out of my skin.

Cross Satan with a chicken and what do you get?
  Devilled eggs.

When the Cyclops visited Paris, what was the first thing he went to see?
  The Eyeffel Tower.

Why did the Cyclops have to stop teaching?
  Because he only had one pupil.

Frankenstein had a great deal of trouble when he went out to buy an electric toothbrush. He didn't know if his teeth were A.C. or D.C. . .

. . . He was advised to visit his dentist at least once a year, and his electrician every six months.

Why couldn't the Bride of Frankenstein use any make-up?
  Every time she tried to put on her face cream, it curdled!

Why did Frankenstein swallow a whole bottle of aspirins?
  He had a monstrous headache.

Why does Frankenstein walk so stiffly?
  Because he put too much starch in his underwear.

When Frankenstein died, his body was taken apart and buried. The tombstone read:
  HERE LIES THE FRANKENSTEIN MONSTER.
  MAY HE RUST IN PIECES.

A monster sheep had an amazing amount of wool on its body. Where did it go to get it cut?
  To the baa baa shop.

Beware of a beautiful witch. She'll sweep you right off your feet.

What do you get if you cross a beautician with a werewolf?
  A monster with beautiful hair—all over its body!

Have you heard the story about the monster peacock?
  It's a beautiful tale (tail).

Why are monster wolves like playing-cards?
  They both come in packs.

What monster birds hover over people lost in the desert?
  Luncheon vultures.

Where does a ten tonne monster sit when he rides on a bus?
  Anywhere he wants to!

What was the monster tortoise doing on the motorway?
  About 200 metres an hour.

Those monster skunks are arguing again—they love to raise a stink!

Fangtastically Funny

Dracula gets lots of cavities because he eats too much chocolate. He's known to have a sweet fang . . .

Dracula complained to Frankenstein, 'My fangs are aching me so—they're driving me to extraction!'

What do you call a school for female monsters?
  An all-ghouls school.

Two creatures from outer space landed by a traffic light.
  'I saw her first,' said one of the creatures.
  'So what?' said the other, 'I'm the one she winked at.'

What did the outer space monster say to the petrol pump?
  'Take your finger out of your ear and listen to me!'

What do you get when you cross a werewolf with a Brontosaurus?
  I'm not sure, but I wouldn't want to be within a thousand miles of it when the moon is full!

There's one job I'd hate to have—being a dog-catcher in Transylvania on nights when the moon is full.

Which disease do ghosts fear the most?
  The **Booo**-bonic plague.

Did you read about the two unmarried ghosts who lived together because they believed in doing what comes supernaturally?

'Do you believe in ghosts?'
    'Of course not.'
    'Would you spend the night in a house that's supposedly haunted?'
    'NO!'
    'Why not?'
    'I might be wrong.'

Just a thought—does Dracula have a wisdom fang?

What's a vampire's worst enemy?
    Fang decay.

'I hear you went to a spiritualist yesterday. How was she?'
    'Oh—just medium.'

What's the first thing a ghost should do when it enters a car?
    Fasten its sheet belt.

Mirage—isn't that where a ghost keeps its car?

First ghost: Where did you go for your holiday?
Second ghost: To the Ritz.
First ghost: Did you? That's one of my favourite haunts.

A group of ghosts got together to protest against air pollution. They held a haunt-in on the grounds of the Houses of Parliament.

What do you get if you cross King Kong with a giant bullfrog?
    A monster that hops up the side of the World Trade Centre and catches aeroplanes with his tongue!

What is big and hairy, wears a dress and climbs up the Empire State Building?
    Queen Kong.

A man complained to a psychiatrist, 'You've got to help me—I keep dreaming of bats, creatures, demons, monsters and vampires.'
    'Very interesting,' remarked the doctor. 'Do you always dream in alphabetical order?'

As monster children get bigger they become increasingly grow-tesque!

How do you greet a two-headed monster from another world?
    You say 'Hello! Hello!'

Dracula is known to love flowers. On Sunday afternoons he can often be seen with his family at the Bat-anical gardens.

King Kong refused to sign another contract with a Hollywood film studio. He was afraid the owner was trying to make a monkey out of him.

What did King Kong say when he heard his sister had a baby?
    'Well—I'll be a monkey's uncle!'

What's the name of the most famous painting found in the pyramids?
    Whistler's mummy.

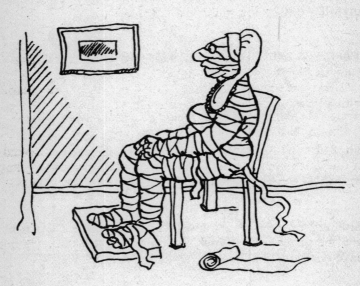

Dracula's son shows signs of becoming a real artist—he loves to draw blood.

When Dracula flew into the home of his favourite victim for the thirteenth time, the man protested saying, 'Look here, Dracula—I'm tired of being stuck for the drinks every night!'

When he's through with one victim and ready for another, Dracula yells, 'Neck-st!'

Waiter to Dracula: Would you like your cup of blood red, or with cream and sugar?

NEWS FLASH

The witches have formed a union and are calling for sweeping reforms!

Dracula had a race with another vampire. It was a neck and neck finish.

A mother ghost brought her child to a doctor. 'Please seewhat's wrong with him,' she pleaded. 'He's always in such good spirits.'

A man was invited to stay the night at an eerie-looking manor house. The butler showed him to his room, which was dark and dirty with cobwebs on the walls.
'I hope you'll be comfortable', said the butler. 'If you need anything during the night just scream.'

What did the monster mother say to her children when they were eating supper?
'How many times do I have to tell you kids—stop eating with your fingers and use the shovel.'

The Martian monster landed in front of a piano shop, looked at one of the open instruments on display and said, 'Okay wise-guy—wipe that smile off your face!'

Another monster who was with him was amazed when he saw the piano keys. 'Wow,' he remarked, 'do these people have dentists!'

Frankenstein walked stiffly into a pub and ordered a coke.
'That will be one pound, please,' said the barman. Then he added, 'We don't get many monsters like yourself coming in here.'
'I'm not surprised,' said the monster, 'with coke a pound a bottle!'

'I'll have to charge you £100 to fill this cavity,' said the dentist to Dracula.
'But that's impossible!' answered Dracula. 'Your rates are only £20 per cavity.'
'Generally that's correct, but as soon as you came into the waiting room you frightened away all my other patients.'

The little monster came home from school in tears. 'Mummy,' he cried 'The children at school all laugh at me. They say my head is too big.'
'Ignore those nasty children and get me a few things at the supermarket,' said the mother. 'I want 15 kg of potatoes, 12 kg of onions, four water-melons, and ten cabbages.'
'Okay, Mum—where's the shopping trolley?'
'It's broken. Just put the things in your cap.'

When Dracula woke up from the anaesthetic, he saw the dental surgeon standing over him.
'I've got some good news and some bad news,' said the dentist. 'First the bad news—I pulled the wrong fang. Now the good news—your other fang doesn't need pulling after all.'

How can you tell whether Dracula has been at your tomato juice?
There'll be two tiny tooth marks on the top of the can.

'Mummy,' said young Dracula, 'That dentist wasn't painless like he advertised.'

'Did he hurt you, dear?'

'No, but he screamed just like any other dentist when I bit his pinky.'

The owner of a cinema in Miami, Florida, felt it was too expensive to install air-conditioning, so he decided to show horror films during the hot summer months. He was hoping that the films would make his audiences' blood run cold!

Murphy the monster came stomping into the kitchen demanding service.

'Where's my food?' he asked. 'And where's my drink? Where's my paper, and where's my. . .'

'Wait a minute,' said his wife. 'Can't you see I've only got five hands?'

Dracula and an Indian were having a rest after giving blood at a clinic.

'Are you a full-blooded Indian?' asked Dracula.

'Usually I am,' replied the Indian, 'but right now I'm a couple of litres short.'

A woman went up to a ghost and asked, 'How much will you charge to give my husband a good fright?'

'For £10,' said the ghost, 'I'll scare him out of his wits.'

'Good,' said the woman. 'Here's £5—he's only a half wit!'

King Kong is going bald—he's going to buy a toupée. Soon he'll be nicknamed Big Wig!

MONSTER TONGUE TWISTER

Repeat ten times fast—*Big Wig*

A little girl was taken to her first seance. The medium asked, 'Is there anyone you would like to talk to?'

'Yes,' said the girl. 'My grandmother.'

The medium closed her eyes for a minute, then all of a sudden a voice spoke.

'Hello, Andrea. This is grandma speaking from heaven.'

'Hi, grandma,' answered the little girl. 'How come you're in heaven? You haven't even died yet!'

A man became the pen friend to a lovely young lady. They exchanged many letters, and finally the woman decided it was time they actually met.

The man wrote, 'I never told you this, but I'm 3 metres tall, with two heads, three eyes, five arms and a scaly body. In short—I'm a monster.'

The young lady wrote back, 'I don't care about your looks. Your letters have meant so much to me, I simply have to meet you.'

'In that case,' wrote the monster, 'I'll meet you Sunday at seven p.m. at Carnegie Hall.

'P.S. I'll wear a red rose in my lapel so you'll be sure to recognize me.'

Four ghosts were playing poker when a fifth ghost opened the door and came in. The wind from the opening and closing of the door blew all the cards off the table. One of the players was obviously annoyed and said, 'Why don't you come in through the keyhole like everyone else?'

A storm was raging over the countryside and lightning brightened up the night sky. Frankenstein thought to himself, 'What a rotten, miserable evening. It makes you feel glad to be alive.'

'You're going to be very happy with the bride I've created for you,' said Dr Frankenstein to his monster. 'She has everything a man like you could ask for—enormous muscles, a deep voice, hairy chest, long beard . . .'

The winner of the Miss Monster World Contest walked on stage, and the announcer said, 'Here she is folks—take a look at those beautiful legs, beautiful legs, beautiful legs. . .'

There's a rumour that Dracula has fallen in love with the girl next door. He took her for a ride in his new bloodmobile and told her, 'I just love your type—RH-negative!'

Wolfman and Dracula were watching a funeral. 'Now that's what I call a sturdy, well-built coffin,' observed Dracula. 'A coffin like that is sure to last a lifetime.'

An old woman was brewing some tea on her lawn when suddenly a flying saucer landed right in the middle of her garden.

Out came a horrible looking creature saying, 'Take me to your leader.'

'Nonsense,' said the woman, 'You should see a good plastic surgeon!'

Dracula's son: All the boys at school tease me—they say I'm a vampire.
Mother: Don't pay any attention to them—they're just ignorant children. Now finish your soup before it clots.

A Martian landed in Las Vegas and watched as people played a slot machine. Finally, after two hours, the Martian walked up to the machine and said, 'I want to shake your hand too.'

MONSTER TONGUE TWISTER

Repeat ten times fast—*Tyrannosaurus Rex*

A man went to see a psychiatrist and complained about having the same terrible nightmare. 'It's horrible,' he said. 'My mother-in-law comes into my bedroom with a hideous monster on a chain. Those red eyes stare at me, the coarse matted hair, giant jaws, long fingernails. . .'

'It sounds beastly,' remarked the psychiatrist.

'Oh, it is,' said the man. 'And that's not all. You should see the monster!'

Frankenstein was discussing his new bride with Dracula. 'Her nose is her best feature. I simply love the way it turns up at the end—then turns down, then sideways, then around, then up again, then. . .'

Ted: Yesterday I took my girl to see the film, Bride of Frankenstein.
Ned: What was she like?
Ted: About 2 metres tall, chalky-white complexion, and extremely ugly.
Ned: That's not what I mean. I already know what your girl-friend looks like.

There's a new film out about Frankenstein's monster which shows him as a sweet and gentle creature. When the movie begins you see the monster looking at a bolt of lightning and calling, 'Mother!'

You Can't Keep a Good Man Down

The cannibal monster arrived home to discover his wife chopping up snakes and a small man. 'Oh no,' he groaned 'Not snake and pygmy pie again!'

'No monster will ever eat me,' boasted the hunter. 'You can't keep a good man down.'

When the hunter failed to return to camp his associate remarked, 'He must have disagreed with something that ate him.'

Monster husband: I don't know what to make for dinner.
Monster wife: Just open a tin of someone.

One monster told his friend, 'I've just captured an actor.'
   'Great news,' said the friend, 'I was just in the mood for a thick ham sandwich.'

Monster husband: How many people are we having for dinner?
Monster wife: Just one each, dear.

What did the angry cannibal monster say to another monster?
   'I have a bone to pick with you!'

What's a cannibal monster?
   Someone who's fed up with people.

First monster: Am I late for dinner?
Second monster: I'm afraid so—everyone's eaten!

A cannibal monster had a Chinese wife who tried never to waste food. Whenever there were any leftovers, she made chap suey!

Monster: How much do you charge for dinner?
Waiter: Five pounds a head.
Monster: Okay—bring me two heads and a mixed salad of fingers and toes.

A big plate of food was served at the monster table. A young monster screamed 'I want the nose! I want the nose!'

Have you heard about the hippie cannibal monster who ate three squares a day?

The monsters were having a party, and one of them was sipping a drink with an eye in it. You might say it was just an eyeball before dinner.

A female cannibal monster went to the jewelry department of Harrods. She asked the salesperson, 'Do you have any nose-bones and matching bone earrings?'

Monster child: Is it proper to eat chicken with the fingers?
Monster mum: No—you should eat the fingers separately.

The cannibal monster mother told her son, 'How many times do I have to tell you—don't speak with someone in your mouth.'

Why did the cannibal monster want to become a detective?
So he could grill all the suspects.

'Better not boil this religious man,' said the cannibal monster to the chef. 'He's a friar.'

Martian: How do you know the astronaut has been eaten?
Friend: I've got inside information.

A Martian had his arm around an astronaut and told his wife, 'I've brought a new friend home for dinner.'
'Fine,' said the wife, 'put him in the deep-freeze and we'll have him next week.'

The first thing that people should teach Martian monsters is to be vegetarians!

Monster chief: What's your occupation?
Captured human: I'm an editor for Ward Lock.
Monster chief: Congratulations—tomorrow you'll be editor-in-chief.

There's a monster cannibal medicine man who can grow hair. Well, he can't exactly grow hair, but he can shrink your head so the little you have looks like more!

'Soon you'll be old enough to marry,' said the cannibal monster to his daughter. 'You've got to start looking for an edible young bachelor.'

For breakfast you'll often find a cannibal monster having coffee and buttered host.

The cannibal monster captured two joke tellers and prepared a special soup with them. You might say they became the laughing stock of the village!

Monster assistant chef: We've captured two navy cooks. Shall I stew both of them?
Monster head chef: No—one's enough. Too many cooks spoil the broth.

On the tombstone of a cannibal monster was inscribed:

HERE LIES CANNIBAL PIKE,
HE NEVER MET A MAN HE DIDN'T LIKE.

An aeroplane had engine trouble, forcing the pilot to bail out over thick jungle territory. Unfortunately for him, he landed plop in the middle of a monster cannibal's pot. When the chief saw the pilot he screamed to his chef, 'What's this flier doing in my soup?'

A monster cannibal was walking through the bush with her son. Suddenly a loud sound came roaring from the sky.
'Don't be frightened,' said the mother. 'It's only an aeroplane.'
'What's an aeroplane?' asked the boy.
'It's something like a lobster,' explained the mother. 'There's a lot you have to throw away, but the insides are delicious.'

A violinist was convinced that music could tame wild monsters. So, violin in hand, he travelled to a place where a group of monsters lived. As soon as he arrived, he took his violin out of the case and began to play. Soon the man was surrounded by the entire tribe—they stood entranced by his wonderful skill. But as he was playing, one of the members of the tribe crept up from behind a bush and speared the violinist right through the heart.
'Why did you do that?' demanded the other monsters. 'His music was beautiful.'
'Eh?' said the killer, cupping his hand to his ear.

'Would you rather have Godzilla or King Kong chase you through the jungle?'
'To be perfectly frank, I'd rather have King Kong chase Godzilla!'

A monster cannibal had finished his studies at Oxford and was returning to his people. On the jet plane taking him home, the stewardess offered him the menu.

'Never mind that,' said the monster, 'just show me the passenger list.'

The Abominable Snowman saw the refrigerator and immediately gave a salute. After all—it was a General Electric!

Which two letters of the alphabet does the Abominable Snowman prefer?
I.C.

What would you do if Godzilla was in front of you at the theatre?
Miss most of the entertainment.

Godzilla's little finger smelled bad. He had a stinky pinky!

MONSTER TONGUE TWISTER

Say ten times fast—*Stinky Pinky*

Cross a zebra with King Kong and what do you get?
A giant ape in a pin-stripe suit.

Just Some Jokes In Bat-taste

What fruit does Dracula prefer?
   Neck-tarines.

When Dracula arrives home, the first thing he puts on is his bat-robe.

What do you call the place where monsters hang out?
   Their terror-tory.

Dracula didn't like his blind date—she wasn't his blood type!

What type of coffee does Dracula drink?
   Neck-afé.

MONSTER TONGUE TWISTER

Say ten times fast—*Dracula Drinks*

Some vampires think that Dracula dresses in very bat-taste.

When Dracula needs a shower he goes into the bat-room.

What did Dracula think of his grandma?
   He felt she was a real old bat!

Young vampires love toys which are run on bat-teries.

Why couldn't young Dracula go to the film?
   He had to stay home and study for his blood test.

What does Jaws like to eat for a snack?
   A peanut-butter-and-jellyfish sandwich.

And Jaws second favourite snack—submarine sandwiches!

Why does the Royal yacht have funny-looking rubber bumpers?
   They're the shark absorbers.

Cross a monster with a parrot and what do you get?
   I don't know, but when it talks you'd better listen!

Why did Jaws get a ticket?
   He was caught in a no-sharking zone.

What did Jaws say when he ran into a school of electric eels?
   Nothing—he was too shocked!

What American city does Jaws want to visit?
   Shark-ago (Chicago).

Why did Jaws cross the road?
   To get to the other tide.

Which author does Jaws love to read?
   William Sharkspeare.

FIENDS, ROMANS, COUNTRYMEN...

Who did Jaws call when his baby grand sounded off key?
   A piano tuna.

'Is it true that a monster won't hurt you if you run away from it?'
'That all depends upon how fast you run!'

What happened to Ray after he tangled with a monster?
He became ex-Ray.

What's it called when the Frankenstein monster plays a joke on you?
A Frank prank.

MONSTER TONGUE TWISTER

Say ten times quickly—*Frank Prank*

The Egyptian monster was so thoughtful—he always sent his mother a Happy Mummy's Day card.

What music do mummies like best?
Ragtime.

MONSTER TONGUE TWISTER

Say ten times fast—*Mummy Mummy*

What street did the mummy live on?
A dead end.

What's the difference between mummies and broken coffins that have been fixed?
Nothing—they are both men dead (mended).

How can you tell who's a real mummy at a masquerade party?
He'll be the one in gauze pyjamas.

Why was the Cyclops jealous of the Mississippi river?
Because it had four eyes (i's)!

How is a Cyclops like the following words: pig, did, lit, tip?
They all have an eye (i) in the middle.

When is a Cyclops' eye not an eye?
When a strong wind makes it water.

What do abominable snowmen prefer—bicycles or tricycles?
Neither—they prefer icicles!

Abominable snowmen can often be heard singing their favourite tune, 'There's no business like snow business. . .'

What do abominable snowmen love to eat?
Chilli.

Where do they keep their money?
In a snowbank.

There once was a Cyclops named Sy,
His head contained just one eye.
  The people who spied Sy
  With not two but one eye
Would sigh to themselves, 'My, oh my!'

MONSTER TONGUE TWISTER

Repeat ten times quickly—*Sighing Cyclops*

Don't make the Abominable Snowman mad—he's dangerous if he gets hot under the collar and loses his cool!

What do you call the cloak that King Kong likes to throw over his shoulders?
An ape cape.

MONSTER TONGUE TWISTER

Repeat ten times quickly—*Ape Cape*

Cross King Kong with a blueberry and what do you get?
A hairy blueberry!

What do you call King Kong's doorbell?
King Kong's ding dong.

What happens when Dracula gets mad?
He sees red.

King Kong likes to play table tennis. Put another way, you could say that King Kong plays ping pong!

MONSTER TONGUE TWISTER

Repeat ten times fast—*King Kong Plays Ping Pong*

What do you call a murderous ape?
A killa gorilla.

What has twenty heads but can't think?
  A book of matches.

Cross a goat and a monster and what do you get?
  An animal that eats a path to your door.

Cross an owl with a monster and you wind up with a bird that frightens people, but doesn't give a hoot!

The apprentice witches are studying hard—soon they'll have to take their final hex-aminations!

Who can join the monsters' PTA?
  Mummies and deadies.

There's a new chocolate bar called Jaws—it costs an arm and a leg!

How does a monster count to 100?
  On his fingers!

How do you cut a dinosaur in two?
  With a dino-saw.

One monster was having her coming out party. But she was so ugly the other monsters made her go in again!

Grave-diggers are truly down-to-earth people.

Which dragon eats with its tail?
  All of them—no dragon removes its tail to eat.

One dragon keeps telling of how great he is. He's a braggin' dragon!

MONSTER TONGUE TWISTER

Repeat ten times fast—*Braggin' Dragon*

What do you call a brave man who puts his right arm into the mouth of Jaws?
  Lefty.

MONSTER TONGUE TWISTER

Repeat ten times fast—*Phony Phantom*

How do witches on broomsticks drink their tea?
  Out of flying saucers.

A female ghost got married. During the wedding she threw
her bridesmaids her **booo**quet.

What day do ghosts prefer?
  Moanday.

*What do you call a clean, well-shaven, hardworking and friendly
monster?*
  A total failure.

A male monster saw a female monster passing by and
remarked 'You have a beautiful pair of legs, pair of legs, pair
of legs.'

What do you call a monster who kills his mother and father?
  An orphan.

*What did Dracula say after he finished biting the young woman's
neck?*
  'It's been nice gnawing you.'

Did you hear about the zombie who swallowed a spoon? He
couldn't stir.

How should you treat a sick monster?
  With respect.

What should you do if King Kong sneezes?
  Get out of the way.

How can you contact Jaws?
  Drop him a line.

When Dr Jekyll wants some privacy, he goes to his
Hyde-a-way.

If two mummies ring your front doorbell what do you have?
  Two dead ringers.

If the stork brings human babies, what brings giant babies?
  Cranes.

Why did the giant monster jog every day?
  To get his extra-size (exercise)!

There's a monster with such a horrible personality that every
time he throws a boomerang it never comes back!

Vampire families are said to be very close—after all, blood is
thicker than water.

The Invisible Man is not very popular with girls at
parties—remember he's not much to look at.

Who won the monster beauty contest?
  No-one!

How did King Kong escape from his cage?
  He used a monkey wrench.

Why is a haunted house like a rabbit farm?
  They're both hair (hare) raising places.

How do you stop an angry monster from charging?
  Take away his credit cards.

What part of this book is like Jaws?
  The fin-ish.

Monsters love necklaces—especially chokers!

You can always tell when a witch is carrying a time
bomb—you can hear their brooms tick!

Young spirits go to an amusement park and spend all their
time riding the roller ghoster (coaster).

Dr Frankenstein often amused his monster—in fact, he kept him in stitches!

Skeletons are like blank applications—their forms haven't filled out.

What do you call a skeleton who's your good friend?
  A bony crony!

MONSTER TONGUE TWISTER

Repeat ten times quickly—*Bony Crony*

Why did the monster go out with a prune?
  He couldn't get a date.

What do monsters have that no-one else has?
  Baby monsters.

What's dangerous and yellow?
  Shark-infested custard.

It's good to tell monster stories in hot weather—after all, they're chilling!

Did you hear about the monster who drank a can of shellac and died?
  He had a fine finish!

Ghostly Gags

When ghosts haunt a theatre the actors usually get stage fright!

When zombies go to the theatre they prefer to view the show from dead centre!

The walking dead got together and started singing, 'Oh what a beautiful mourning (morning). . .'

Where do cowboy spirits live?
  In a ghost town.

Cross a werewolf with a boat and what do you get?
  A wolf in ships clothing.

Young monsters go to monster school and are taught by a creature teacher.

MONSTER TONGUE TWISTER

Repeat ten times fast—*Creature Teacher*

There's a new science fiction film with the same old plot—boy meets girl, boy loses girl, boy builds new girl . . .

In order to prevent disease, young ghost children have to have their **booo**-ster shots.

What happened to the wolf who fell into the washing machine?
He became a wash-and-werewolf.

What do you get by crossing a monster with a cat?
A neighbourhood without dogs.

Cross a monster with a Boy Scout and what do you get?
A monster who's always prepared.

Skeletons are usually quite calm—after all, nothing ever gets under their skin.

What's King Kong's favourite flower?
Chimp-pansies.

In what way is a monster good-looking?
Away-off!

Which side of a werewolf has the most hair?
The outside.

What's the difference between a werewolf and a flea?
A werewolf can have fleas but a flea can't have werewolves.

Dragons are never to be believed—remember, they're full of hot air.

What do you call a monster lobster that refuses to share its food?
A selfish shellfish.

MONSTER TONGUE TWISTER

Repeat ten times fast—*Selfish Shellfish*

Jaws was slightly deaf. What did he have to use?
A herring (hearing) aid.

How can you tell a shark from spaghetti?
A shark won't slip off the end of your fork.

What did the little pharaoh say to the monster?
'You'd better leave me alone or I'll tell my mummy.'

How do monsters keep their hair in place?
With scare (hair) spray.

Do people who see ghosts lose their sense of humour?
Yes—they're scared out of their wits.

What sound do two vampires make when they kiss?
Ouch!

What kind of dates do ghouls go out with?
Anybody they can dig up!

What's the best present to give a witch for her birthday?
A charm bracelet.

It's no wonder that mummies are often nervous—they're all wound up!

How is an evil witch like a candle?
They are both wick-ed.

What terrible female creature can be found in lunch boxes?
Sandwitches (sandwiches).

What do you call monster cattle?
Mon-steers.

Why do skeletons catch cold faster than any other creature?
Because they get chilled to the bone!

Where did the sick monster go?
To a witchdoctor.

How does Count Dracula travel?
By blood vessel.

Werewolves should become comedians—after all, they're a howl.

Where are werewolves sent who won't behave properly?
To obedience school.

Knock! Knock!
Who's there?
Egypt.
Egypt who?
Egypt me—I want my mummy back.

MONSTER TONGUE TWISTER

Repeat ten times fast—*Sixty-six Skeletons*

What vegetable do you get when a giant monster walks through your garden?
　Squash!

Cross a pile of hay with a vampire and what do you get?
　A bale O'Lugosi (Bela Lugosi).

What's the difference between a hungry monster and a greedy monster?
　One longs to eat, the other eats too long.

What do you call a monster who's 3 metres tall?
　Shorty.

Cross King Kong with a skunk and what do you get?
　A great big stink.

What famous play about monsters was written by William Shakespeare?
　Romeo and Ghouliet.

What did the monster say to the scarecrow?
　'I can beat the stuffin' out of you.'

Dracula's wife told him, 'Go brush your teeth—you have very bat-breath.'

Cross King Kong with a parrot and what do you get?
　A lot of big talk.

Do you know what they call a skeleton that talks all the time?
　A jaw-bone.

A cowardly sea serpent is known as chicken of the sea!

Dracula's been ordered by his doctor to try to take it easy and calm down—apparently he's developed high blood pressure.

Do you know what will happen if Dracula bites you? You'll get a drain in the neck!

Cross a skunk with Godzilla and what do you get?
　A monster skunk that smells awful?

Always be certain to pay your exorcist promptly—otherwise, you may get repossessed.

What did the monster cannibal say after he ate ten people?
　Burp!

What made the ghost so annoyed?
  His new sheet shrunk in the laundry.

MONSTER TONGUE TWISTER

Repeat ten times fast—*Shrunk Sheet*

What do you call a swarm of monster bees?
  Zombees.

MONSTER TONGUE TWISTER

Repeat ten times fast—*Tom Bee the Zombee*

Jim: What do dragons do to get rid of their frustrations?
Tim: They let off steam!

What do Dracula's children love to eat?
  Fang-furters.

Jaws is a man-eating monster shark. Who is safe from him?
  Women and children.

Did you hear about the woman who gave birth to a
monstrous-looking child? It was so ugly that instead of
slapping the baby, the doctor slapped the mother!

Zombies like sweets, but they never eat life-savers!

When do two-headed monsters do well at school?
  When they use their heads.

Do you know how to make a skeleton laugh?
  It's easy—just tickle it's funny bone.

What's Dracula's favourite sport?
  Skin diving.

One monster snake telephoned his friend in another part of
the country. They spoke poison-to-poison!

What type of dinosaur does a cowboy ride in a rodeo?
  A bucking bronco-saurus.

MONSTER TONGUE TWISTER

Repeat ten times fast—*Bucking Bronco-saurus*

As a child Jaws went to school. When he learned how to dive
to the ocean floor he was given a deep-loma (diploma).

What's worse than seeing Jaw's fin in the water?
  Seeing his throat.

What monster is green, has a cape, and comes out in the night?
  A vampickle!

*When werewolves want to fight for their country what do they
join?*
  The hair force (Air force).

What does Frankenstein think of this book?
  He says it's electrifying.

The monster's girl-friend has pedestrian eyes. They can look
both ways before they cross!

'Mummy, Mummy—when will you buy a rubbish bin?'
  'Shut up and keep eating!'

What television programme does Jaws like to watch?
  Name that tuna.

What do you call a nervous witch?
  Twitch.

MONSTER TONGUE TWISTER

Repeat ten times fast—*Witch with twitch*

Who was gigantically tall and laughed a lot?
   The jolly green giant.

If Jaws became a waiter what might he say to a customer?
   'At Jaw service.'

What monster was a famous explorer?
   Christopher Ghoulumbus (Columbus).

Cross a rooster with King Kong and what do you get?
   The biggest cluck in town.

'That monster keeps double-talking.'
   'Well, what do you expect from someone with four lips?'

What weighs 1,000 kg, but is all bone?
   A skele-tonne.

Why is Dracula slowing down?
   Tired blood.

Cemeteries are popular places—people are dying to get in!

What did Dracula use to brush his teeth?
   Fangpaste.

Monstrous Mirth

How do you make a thin monster fat?
   Throw him up into the air and he'll come down 'plump'!

Where can an ugly monster go if he wants to find sympathy?
   To the dictionary.

The Frankenstein monster loved lightning—it gave him a big charge!

Cross a vampire with a snowball and what do you get?
   Frostbite.

Cannibal monster mother: What are you doing, Junior?
Junior: Chasing the man around the tree.
Mother: How many times have I told you not to play with your food?

Did you hear about the werewolf who went to the flea circus?
   He stole the show.

Why couldn't the midget lend the giant monster ten pounds?
   Because he was terribly short.

What's the hardest thing facing a monster man on the flying trapeze?
   The floor.

What happened to the teeny weeny monsters that applied for a job at the circus?
   They were put on the short list.

'Did you hear about the monster's child who ran away with the circus.'
'No—what happened?'
'The police made him bring it back!'

I've just seen a monster musician with 100 fingers—what a pianist!

Frankenstein took young Dracula to the zoo and they started feeding the monkeys—they started feeding them to the lions!

One monstrous-looking girl is so ugly, every time she visits the freak show at the circus she has to buy two tickets—one to get in and one to get out!

Did you hear about the three-year-old boy whose mother took him to a freak show? No matter how she pleaded they still wouldn't have him!

Sharing a meal with horrible-looking monsters changes the law of gravity—what goes down must come up!

Teachers at school told Dracula that his son should go far—they recommended Uranus.

There's a monster who is so old that when he was at school history was called current events!

Father: What do you mean the school must be haunted?
Son: Well, the headmaster keeps talking about the school spirit.

What does Dracula think of this book?
He says, so far it's fangtastic!

Cross a pet dog and a werewolf and what do you get?
A new owner every full moon!

How do you use an Egyptian mummy's doorbell?
Toot and come in (Tutankamen).

'How did you feel after the monster knocked you about?'
'Absolutely whacked!'

'You're a pretty dirty monster,' said the teacher.
'Yes,' answered the female ghoul. 'And I'm even prettier when I'm clean.'

Dracula: What did you learn in school today?
Young Dracula: Not enough—I have to go back tomorrow.

Monster child: I put a bomb under the teacher's chair.
Father: 'You naughty boy—go back to school and remove it at once.
Monster child: What school!

What did Dracula say when he was stabbed through the heart with a stake?
  'Ouch!'

Did you hear what happened after King Kong got married?
  Months later his wife gave birth to a giant banana!

When werewolf acted as old St Nick, he was known as Santa Claws!

Cross a cocker spaniel, a poodle and a ghost and what do you get?
  A cock-a-poodle-*booo*!

MONSTER TONGUE TWISTER

Repeat ten times fast—*Cock-a-poodle-booo*

How can you tell when a giant monster is under your bed?
  Your nose will be touching the ceiling.

What monster was round and purple and ruled Russia?
  Peter the Grape.

Name the monster mouse who was a Roman Emperor.
  Julius Cheeser.

How did the Baron decide to build the Frankenstein monster?
  It came to him in a flash.

What do you call a skeleton who's always telling lies?
A bony phony.

MONSTER TONGUE TWISTER

Repeat ten times fast—*Bony Phony*

What monster fowl conquered half the world?
Attila the hen.

The creator of Frankenstein put dynamite in his fridge.
Apparently, he lost his cool!

Where do Martian monsters leave their space ships?
At parking meteors.

A Martian monster visiting earth took this book back with
him to Mars, and couldn't put it down!

*What problem did Martian monsters have when they arrived on
Earth?*
They weren't sure who were the people and who were the
pets.

Why do Martian monsters prefer pubs here on Earth?
Because they have much more atmosphere.

*Why should you wear dark glasses when having a conversation
with Martian monsters?*
Because they're all so bright.

*What present might you give a Martian monster to keep his hands
warm?*
Ten pairs of gloves.

*What happened to the unbreakable shock-proof, water-proof
anti-magnetic watch that the monster received for Christmas?*
He lost it.

What monster fish terrorizes others in the sea?
Jack the Kipper.

How do monster children learn to get what they want?
By trial and terror.

Did you hear about the monster thief who was allergic to prison?
Every time they put him in a cell, he started to break out!

Do you know what vampire sailors call their ships?
Blood vessels.

A monster who looks like a bear
Fell soundly asleep in a chair.
   He woke with loud screaming
   Because he was dreaming
That barbers had shaved off his hair!

A very ugly monstrocity
Wanted a look of ferocity.
   With his nose in the air
   He walked like a bear,
Which only suggested pomposity.

There are monster musicians galore.
Someday there'll be quite a few more.
   Their numbers increased
   And none are deceased,
They now total 10,004.

What famous vampire lives in Tibet?
   Count Yakula.

There once was a yeti named Netty
Who lived with a yeti named Betty.
   Each time that they'd meet
   They'd go out to eat
Their favourite—uncooked spaghetti!

When Dracula has gas in his stomach he's known as a
cramp-ire!

What do you call a vampire who sleeps rough?
   A tramp-ire!

A monster child named Molly
Played with her new Christmas dolly.
   While playing with dolly
   She sucked on a lolly,
Molly was jolly by golly.

'Daddy, Daddy—come quick! Mummy's fighting a massive
monster!'
   'Don't worry—I'm sure the monster can take care of
himself.'

There's a new film about the Lock Ness monster and Jaws.
It's called Lock Jaws!

Cross a snail with Dracula and what do you get?
   The world's slowest flying vampire!

The warlock could sculpture all kinds of wonderful
things from skull-bone. He had a high degree of
witchcraftsmanship.

What do you call a one-eyed monster on a motorbike?
  A Cycle-ops.

What do you call a ghost doctor?
  A surgical spirit.

What music do mummies like best?
  Ragtime.

MONSTER TONGUE TWISTER

Say ten times fast—*Mummy Mummy*

What form of transport does a sorceress prefer?
  Witchcraft.

To a witch, hex marks the spot.

A warlock met a witch and wanted to take her home. He said, 'Shall we walk or hail a broom?'

Instead of walking the warlock and his girl tried to thumb a ride. In other words, they witch-hiked!

Gory Stories

What do vampires call a coffin?
  A snuff box.

The Baron von Frankenstein was a lonely man until he
learned how to make friends!

Baron von Frankenstein told his estate agent, 'Please find me
a new house—not too big—just big enough to hang my hat
and a few friends!'

'Doctor, doctor, every night I dream there are horrible green
monsters under my bed. What shall I do?'
  'Saw the legs off your bed.'

King Kong's grandson is gaining weight. He's now a chunky
monkey.

MONSTER TONGUE TWISTER

Say ten times fast—*Chunky Monkey*

Godzilla: I think I'll eat the city of Hong Kong. Would you
care to join me for dinner?
King Kong: No thanks—I don't care for Chinese food.

'I didn't come to Earth to be insulted!' said the Martian
monster.
  'No—where do you usually go?' asked the Earthman.

A young woman married a ghost, then told her family, 'I can't think what possessed me to do it.'

Did you hear about the monster who was kind, loveable, considerate . . . wait a minute—this story is in the wrong jokebook!

'I don't think these photos you took do me justice,' said the hideous-looking monster.
  'You don't want justice,' said the photographer, 'What you want is mercy!'

'I understand you buried your pet monster last week.'
  'Had to—dead you know.'

Dracula: Why are you so angry?
Wolfman: It's all the rage!

'My girl-friend's one of twins.'
  'How can you tell them apart?'
  'She's the one with the beard.'

Dracula: Tomorrow you will fly solo.
Dracula's son: How low?

'That monster looks like Helen Green.'
  'Yes—and she looks even worse in red!'

Wolfman went with Dracula to explore a cave. . .
Wolfman: Dark in here isn't it?
Dracula: I don't know—I can't see to tell.

Dracula: Why are you jumping up and down young Dracula?
Dracula's son: I just took some medicine and I forgot to shake the bottle!

Young Dracula: This morning Mum gave Dad some soap-flakes for breakfast.
Wolfman: He must have been mad.
Young Dracula: Mad—he was foaming at the mouth!

There once was a monster squid
Who ate twenty kids for a quid.
  When asked, 'Are you faint?'
  He replied, 'No I ain't,
Though I don't feel as well as I did!'

A female monster went into a dress shop. 'Can I try the dress on in the window?'
  'No,' said the salesperson. 'I don't care if you are a monster—you'll have to use the changing-room like everyone else!'

Dracula: Just look at you—you're full of bruises. What happened?
Wolfman: I started to walk through a revolving door and then I changed my mind.

'Where should I meet you?' asked the boy ghost to the girl ghost.
'Under the clothes-line,' she answered. 'That's where I hang out!'

An old witch said to Dr Jekyll, 'Some men think I'm pretty and others think I'm ugly. What do you think?'
'A bit of both,' answered Dr Jekyll. 'Pretty ugly!'

Frankenstein: When's your birthday?
Young Dracula: 6th April.
Frankenstein: What year?
Young Dracula: Every year!

The Abominable Snowman was asked by another monster, 'Where's your Mum from?'
'Alaska,' he replied.
'Don't bother,' said the monster, 'I'll ask her myself!'

The son of the Abominable Snowman went ice-fishing, and do you know what?
He brought home 100 kg of ice!

What does a Chinese monster drive?
A Rolls Rice.

'A noise woke me up this morning,' said Dr Jekyll to his secretary.
'Really? What was it,' he asked.
'The crack of dawn,' came the reply.

A lazy monster got a job in a bakery. He thought it would be the perfect place for a good loaf.

The Devil laughed out loud when Dracula told him about an angel who died of harp failure!

A female skeleton got engaged to a male skeleton, then discovered he had a wooden leg. She broke it off, of course.

Dracula's very polite—after he bites his victims he always says, 'Fang you very much!'

What's covered with ribbons and bows and comes from outer space?
   A gift-wrapped Martian.

If a Martian monster aims his death-ray gun at you, what's better than presence of mind?
   Absence of body.

How do Martian monsters drink their tea?
   From flying saucers.

Martian monster: Are you tanned from the sun?
Astronaut: No—I'm Harry from the Earth.

How can you arrange a trip to Mars to visit the monsters?
   You planet (plan it).

Two outer space monsters were thirsty and landed their space ship on the Pacific Ocean. One of the monsters told the other, 'You can drink first but leave some for me.'

What did the woman say when she gave birth to Siamese twins?
   'They'll be the smartest kids in the class—after all, two heads are better than one!'

When are soldiers like outer space monsters?
    When they're Martian along.

What did the Martian say when he landed in the field of weeds?
    'Take me to your weeder.'

Dracula: What's the difference between a witch and a snoo?
Wolfman: What's snoo?
Dracula: Nothing—what's snoo with you?

What do Martian children love to eat?
    Martian-mellows.

What do you get when a rooster fights a monster?
    Creamed chicken.

What's the difference between children at Christmas and werewolves?
    Werewolves have claws on their fingers while kids at Christmas have claws (Claus) on their minds.

'Where are you Ivan?'
    'Here in the closet.'
    'Why are you in there?'
    'You told me to read Dr Jekyll and Hyde!'

There's a new book out called *How To Shoot Space Monsters* by Ray Gun.

Another book by the same publisher is, *A Tourists Guide To Transylvania* by Bee Ware.

When will a monster mathematician die?
    When his number's up.

Cross a computer with a vampire and what do you get?
    Love at first byte.

How can you electrify a vampire?
    With a bat-tery.

Cross the Invisible Man with a cow and what do you get?
    Vanishing cream.

What do you get if you cross a monster frog with a soft drink?
    Croak-a-cola.

What's the most important rule for any monster to learn in chemistry?
    Never lick the spoon.

What kind of typewriter does Dracula use?
  One that types blood.

Cross an oil can with King Kong and what do you get?
  A grease monkey.

What do you call a ghost that's not interested in frightening people?
  A failure!

What does a monster travelling through space do when he gets dirty?
  He takes a meteor shower.

What's round and purple, orbits the sun and has strange fruit monsters living on it?
  Planet of the Grapes.

How do you travel to the planet of the Apes?
  By banana boat.

Why did the warlock pinch the waitress?
  He wanted to see some flying saucers.

Why do monsters from outer space wear bullet-proof vests?
  To protect themselves against shooting stars.

Doctor: Nurse—did you take Dracula's temperature?
Nurse: No—is it missing?

Nurse: Dr Jekyll—why do you always wear a tuxedo in the operating room?
Dr Jekyll: I like to dress formally for openings.

When the monster canary felt sick, where did he go?
  To the doctor for tweetment.

Cross a ballpoint pen with a monstrous giant and what do you get?
  The Ink-credible Hulk.

Cross a loud speaker with a monstrous giant and what do you get?
  Stone deaf!

Cross a stone and a shark and what do you get?
  Rockjaws!

Cross a monster rabbit with a comic and what do you get?
  A funny bunny that walks on its hind legs!

What do you call the cloak that King Kong likes to throw over his shoulders?
An ape cape.

MONSTER TONGUE TWISTER

Repeat ten times fast—*Ape Cape*

What did Whistler's mother do when she saw Dracula flying towards her?
She went off her rocker.

Cross a giant chicken and a cement truck and what do you get?
A hen that lays pavements.

How do you fix a robot in the shape of King Kong?
With a monkey wrench.

Why did Frankenstein visit a psychiatrist?
Because he felt he had a screw loose.

Have you read the book *There Is A Lock Ness Monster* by Y. Knott?

How did the Abominable Snowman make antifreeze?
He put ice cubes in her bed.

Cross a clock with a monster rooster and what do you get?
An alarm cluck.

When King Kong feels sorry for something he did he offers an ape-ology.

Did you hear about the football coach who went into space searching for monsters? He wanted to put together an All-star Team.

Cross a comedian with a spiritualist and what do you get?
A happy medium.

Why wouldn't the Baron ever cross the Frankenstein monster with anything?
Because Frankenstein didn't like to be crossed.

Abominable Snowman: What do you mean by telling everyone I'm an idiot?
Dracula: I'm sorry—I didn't know it was supposed to be a secret.

King Kong once got so mad he was struck with a sudden case of ape-oplexy!

King Kong said, 'These jokes about me are simply ape-alling!'

Young Frankenstein: What did you get for Christmas?
Young Dracula: A kit of drums—and it's the best present I ever got.
Young Frankenstein: Why?
Young Dracula: Because Dad gives me five pounds a week not to play it!

Wolfman: Do you have any invisible ink?
Invisible Man: Certainly—what colour?

Young Dracula: In the park this morning I was surrounded by lions.
Dracula: Lions! In the park?
Young Dracula: Yes—dandelions!

First Dragon: I thought you weren't going to smoke any more.
Second Dragon: I'm not.
First Dragon: But you're smoking as much as ever.
Second Dragon: Well, that's not more is it?

Wolfman: Why are you laughing?
Dracula: My dentist just pulled out one of my fangs.
Wolfman: Is that something to laugh at?
Dracula: Well—it was the wrong fang!

Wolfman: Are you superstitious?
Dracula: No.
Wolfman: Good—then lend me thirteen pounds.

Dr Jekyll: Answer the phone.
Nurse: But it's not ringing.
Dr Jekyll: That's just like you—always leaving things till the last moment.

On the golf course. . .

Dr Jekyll: Good lord—I just sank a hole-in-one.
Dracula: Do it again, I wasn't looking.

Dr Jekyll's son: What's a caddie?
Dr Jekyll: That's a man who follows his work schedule to a tee!

'But Mummy—I don't want to go to France.'
  'Shut up and start swimming!'

Why was the Egyptian child worried?
  Because it's daddy was a mummy.

Why did Grandpa vampire put wheels on his rocking-chair?
  Because he wanted to Rock-n-roll!

'King Kong Junior—it's time for your violin lesson.'
  'Oh, fiddle!'

Why did Godzilla put a snake in his mother's bed?
  Because he couldn't find a crocodile.

Bride of Frankenstein: Will you love me when I'm old and ugly?
Frankenstein: Darling, of course I do.

Dracula's wife: What would you like for your birthday?
Dracula: A tie to match the colour of my eyes.
Wife: But where can I find a bloodshot tie?

Godzilla: Last night my son fell out of the window.
King Kong: Did he hurt himself?
Godzilla: Not at all—we live in a basement flat.

Young Dracula: Dad—there's a man at the front door collecting for the new community swimming pool.
Dracula: Give him a glass of water.

Abominable Snowman: Do you have holes in your underwear?
Godzilla: Of course not.
Abominable Snowman: Then how do you get your arms and feet through?

NEWS FLASH

The grave diggers have just gone on strike. They're demanding a living wage!

Godzilla: Is it true you can jump off a high snowy mountain and not hurt yourself?
Abominable Snowman: No—that's just a bluff.

Godzilla's son: My father baths twice a week.
Dr Jekyll's son: Well, my father baths three times a week.
King Kong's son: That's nothing—my father keeps himself so clean he never has to bath!

Dracula's daughter: Would you like to see my birthmark?
Wolfman's son: How long have you had it?

Godzilla told King Kong: 'Every time I go on a ferry, it makes me cross!'

Why did the monster lobster get a divorce?
She discovered she was married to a crab!

Dracula: Do you think it will rain today?
Dr Jekyll: That all depends on the weather.

Frankenstein: How do you like living in a tent?
Incredible Hulk: There's no room to complain.

In what fight did the Martian monster cry, 'I die happy'?
In his last fight.

Warlock: How did you cure your son of biting his nails?
Wolfman: I knocked out all his teeth!

King Kong's son told Dracula's son, 'When I grow up I'm going to own a huge house with no bathrooms—I'm going to be filthy rich!'

Dracula has graduated with a B.A. degree—a *Bat*chelor of Arts.

Dracula: Every time I'm down in the dumps I buy a new cape.
Wolfman: So that's where you get your capes!

First monster: What's your new boy-friend like?
Second monster: He's mean, selfish, nasty, dirty—and those are just his good points!

Dracula: Your face is clean, but how did you get your hands so dirty?
Dracula's son: Washing my face.

Mother monster: How is my son doing in class?
Teacher: From the quality of his work he should grow up to be an M.D.
Mother monster: You mean a doctor?
Teacher: No—Mentally Deficient!

Monster kid: How many sums did I get right out of 100?
Teacher: All of them—except 99.

Teacher: I checked your homework and the handwriting looks just like your father's.
Young Dracula: Of course it does—I used his pencil.

Teacher: If you had five chocolate bars and your youngest brother asked you for one, how many would you have left?
Son of Frankenstein: Five.

What did one witch say to the other witch when inviting her to supper?
  'You'll just have to take pot luck.'

What did the monster crow say to her nestlings?
  'If you gotta crow, you gotta crow.'

Believe it or not, one monster died, went to heaven, and became an angel. He'd sit on a cloud and greet all the newcomers by saying, 'Halo there!'

What do monster ants take when they're ill?
  Antibiotics.

What do monster bees take when they're ill?
  Anti**bee**otics.

Did you hear about the stupid monster who tried to blow up a bus?
  He burnt his lips on the exhaust pipe.

What did the boy moon monster say to the girl moon monster?
  'Let's take a stroll—there's a beautiful earth out tonight.'

Monsters from outer space are star-craving mad!

Young Frankenstein: I failed every subject but Spanish.
Young Dracula: What did you get in Spanish?
Young Frankenstein: I didn't take Spanish!

One monster got a job as an elevator operator. When asked if he liked his work he said: 'It has its ups and downs.'

Name a monster insect from outer space.
 Bug Rogers.

What did the earthling say to the Martian monster?
 'You're no earthly good.'

Martian science teacher: What is an atom?
Martian pupil: Isn't that the earthling who lived with Eve in the Garden of Eden?

Martian monster kid: Can I watch the eclipse of the Earth?
Martian mother: All right—but don't stand too close.

Martian kid: I've taken this television from Earth apart and put it back together again.
Martian father: Well done—I hope you haven't lost any parts.
Martian kid: Oh no—but I've got about eleven bits left over.

Martian kid: What happens if I swallow uranium?
Martian mother: You'll get atomic ache.

Did the skeleton enjoy the Hallowe'en party?
 Yes—he had a rattling good time.

Beware of toothless vampires. They can't bite—but they can give you a nasty suck!

What do zombies put on their roast beef?
 Grave-y.

What's Dracula's favourite pudding?
 Leeches and scream.

And what's his favourite breakfast?
 Readyneck.

Why did the baby monster push his father's fingers into the light socket?
 He wanted fizzy pop!

Name the sea monster's favourite football team.
  Slitherpool.

What do you call twin ghosts who keep ringing doorbells?
  Dead ringers.